Not Me, Not Now. Mastering Your Time, Your Team, and Yourself

A Simple Guide to Effective Management

Steven Bradley

Copyright © 2023 Steven Bradley

All rights reserved.

ISBN: 9798852789020

CONTENTS

Introduction	1
Chapter One: Lists: Where to Start	3
Chapter Two: Nine Minutes a Day: The Value of Planning Your Goals	6
Chapter Three: Eat Your Veggies First: Prioritization Tips for Success	10
Chapter Four: Two Simple Phrases for Time Management: Not Me, Not Now	13
Chapter Five: Eight Days a Week: The Benefits of Working Efficiently	17
Chapter Six: Be Proactive	21
Chapter Seven: Management Styles Applied	24
Chapter Eight: Leading from Anywhere	30
Chapter Nine: Six Things I Learned from Nehemiah	36
Chapter Ten: Manage, Coach, or Mentor. A Tugboat Story.	39
Chapter Eleven: It's Not Easy Being Green: Tips for New Managers	42
Chapter Twelve: Seven Deadly Manager Sins	46

Not Me, Not Now. Mastering Your Time, Your Team, and Yourself

A Simple Guide to Effective Management

Chapter Thirteen: Your Reputation and Relationships: Protect Them!	51
Chapter Fourteen: Reinvent Yourself, Regularly	54
Summary	57
Acknowledgement	59

INTRODUCTION

When I set out to create a simple document to outline what I've learned about management and leadership over the years I found that list kept getting longer and longer. As someone who has managed people, programs, and processes I have come to appreciate a simplified set of examples that I can use and incorporate into my methodologies. This guide is meant to do that for experienced managers looking to change things up as well as new managers wondering where to get started. It is not meant to be an exhaustive and detailed review of the various methodologies and tools for management but rather a simplified pocket guide to share insights from my experiences. This guide is a compilation of various documents, presentations, and concepts I have discovered and developed over the years. I have leveraged a few Internet resources like Wikipedia, Answers.com, and ChatGPT as research tools to help with definitions and to organize the content.

Not Me, Not Now. Mastering Your Time, Your Team, and Yourself

A Simple Guide to Effective Management

The goal of this guide is to provide simple tips, benefits and insights into time management, people management, and self-management. I have used examples, where appropriate, from my experience to drive home a few points. Some chapters and concepts overlap but each are meant to stand alone. My hope is that as you read each chapter you will discover elements that you can work into your management approach to master your time, your team and yourself.

CHAPTER ONE
LISTS: WHERE TO START

I love lists. Checking things off a list gives one a sense of accomplishment. The only thing better than a simple list is a master list! Master lists are great for capturing the things you need to get done and organizing those tasks, prioritizing them, and setting target dates is helpful to ensure you stay on track. Building good lists begins with understanding the fundamentals of the things that need to get done supporting the major activities and tasks you have assigned. For example, if you want to make an omelet you will need to build a simple list of activities and resources to make the omelet. While this may seem very simple and not worthy of consideration, it is imperative that we all understand what it really takes to accomplish an objective. As a manager or leader in your company/organization you need to understand what it takes to accomplish that objective, who you're assigning it to, and what skills and capabilities they possess.

Constructing well organized lists can help to ensure readiness and your ability to react. However, lists are even more effective for being proactive.

Lists can be a powerful tool for getting organized and staying on top of tasks, responsibilities, and goals. In this chapter, we'll explore how to use lists effectively to improve productivity and manage your time more efficiently.

Make a To-Do List

A to-do list is a simple yet effective way to keep track of the tasks and responsibilities you need to complete. When creating a to-do list, start by identifying the most important tasks and prioritize them accordingly. Break down larger tasks into smaller, more manageable steps, and estimate the time required to complete each task. Be realistic and specific when setting deadlines and focus on completing one task at a time.

Create a Checklist

A checklist is another useful tool for staying organized and ensuring that important tasks are completed properly. For example, you might create a checklist for a specific project or task, outlining the specific steps that need to be completed and the order in which they need to be completed. This can help ensure that no steps are missed and that the project is completed correctly and on time.

Use a Calendar

A calendar is a great way to keep track of deadlines, appointments, and important dates. When using a calendar, make sure to prioritize important tasks and schedule time for them accordingly. Consider using color-coding or other visual cues to make it easier to differentiate between different types of tasks or events.

Create a Master List

A master list is a comprehensive list of all your tasks and responsibilities, including both short-term and long-term goals. This can help you keep track of everything you need to do and prioritize tasks accordingly. Consider using different categories or labels to help you organize tasks and focus on what's most important.

Keep a Notepad Handy

A notepad or notebook can be a useful tool for capturing ideas, thoughts, and reminders throughout the day. Always keep a notepad handy, whether it's a physical notebook or a digital app, so you can jot down ideas and tasks as they come to you. This can help prevent important tasks from slipping through the cracks and ensure that you stay organized and productive.

On the whole, using lists can be an effective way to get organized and stay on top of tasks and responsibilities. By creating a to-do list, checklist, calendar, master list, and keeping a notepad handy, you can improve productivity and manage your time more efficiently. So, start using lists today to get organized and achieve your goals!

CHAPTER TWO
NINE MINUTES A DAY: THE VALUE OF PLANNING YOUR GOALS

Several years ago, I had a team member that was having a difficult time staying focused and completing his assignments on time. To help him get a handle on all his responsibilities I decided to add one more to his list, taking time daily to plan and document his goals. I had him send me a list of his planned and accomplished goals at the beginning and end of every day. This went on for several weeks and occasionally my team member would ask when he could stop sending me updates. I said, "When you no longer think to ask to stop sending updates." After a few more weeks and some healthy "ribbing" from his colleagues about having to do these extra steps every day, he finally got it. I know this because he stopped asking how much longer he'd have to do it and when asked how it was going, he said, "It's almost automatic and it takes less than 10 minutes each day." It was then that I knew I was on to something. Less than 10 minutes a day.

Taking just nine minutes a day to plan your daily goals can have a significant impact on your success and overall well-being. In this chapter, we'll explore the value of taking nine minutes a day to plan your goals and how it can benefit you in all areas of your life. Keep in mind that the main point of this chapter is the idea that taking time at the beginning of your day to plan out all the activities and tasks will allow you to quickly execute on them. Over time you will be able to see patterns in your activities and become more efficient in tackling them. Using this time will help you see the differences in your regular activities so you can set priorities for the day.

Clarity and Focus

When you take the time to plan your goals, you gain clarity and focus on what you want to achieve. You're able to break down your larger goals into smaller, more manageable tasks, making it easier to stay focused and on track. This clarity and focus can help you achieve your goals more efficiently and effectively.

Increased Motivation

When you have a clear plan for achieving your goals, you're more motivated to work towards them. You'll have a sense of direction and purpose, which can help you stay motivated even when the going gets tough. This increased motivation can help you overcome obstacles and achieve your goals more quickly.

Better Time Management

Taking nine minutes a day to plan your goals can also help you manage your time more effectively. By breaking down your goals into smaller tasks, you can prioritize your time and focus on what's most important. This can help you make the most of your time and avoid wasting time on tasks that don't contribute to your goals.

Greater Productivity

When you have a clear plan for achieving your goals and prioritize your time effectively, you'll be more productive. You'll be able to work more efficiently and accomplish more in less time. This increased productivity can help you achieve your goals more quickly and free up time for other activities.

Improved Decision Making

When you have a clear plan for achieving your goals, you'll be better equipped to make decisions that align with your goals. You'll be able to evaluate options more effectively and make decisions that support your long-term objectives. This can help you avoid making decisions that are not in your best interest and stay on track towards your goals.

Reduced Stress

When you have a clear plan for achieving your goals, you'll be less likely to feel overwhelmed and stressed out. You'll have a sense of direction and purpose, which can help you feel more in control of your life. This can lead to reduced stress and improved overall well-being.

Greater Success

By taking nine minutes a day to plan your goals, you'll be more likely to achieve success in all areas of your life. You'll be able to identify and prioritize your goals, stay focused and motivated, and manage your time more effectively. This can lead to greater success in your career, relationships, and personal life.

Increased Self-Awareness

When you take the time to plan your goals, you'll become more self-aware. You'll be able to identify your strengths and weaknesses and develop strategies to overcome obstacles and achieve your goals. You'll be able to identify where you need to focus and where you'll need help. This increased self-awareness can help you grow as a person and become more successful in all areas of your life.

Improved Well-Being

Taking nine minutes a day to plan your goals can improve your overall well-being. You'll have a sense of purpose and direction, reduced stress, and greater success in all areas of your life. This can lead to improved physical and mental health, and a more fulfilling life.

The amount of time that you spend in daily planning isn't important. Why did I choose nine minutes? No particular reason other than to suggest a little time planning each day's activities promises to be valuable. And, considering all these benefits, taking just nine minutes a day to plan your goals can have a significant impact on your success and overall well-being. By gaining clarity and focus, increasing motivation, improving time management, and making better decisions, you'll be more likely to achieve your goals and live a fulfilling life. At least one day at a time.

CHAPTER THREE
EAT YOUR VEGGIES FIRST: PRIORITIZATION TIPS FOR SUCCESS

There's a saying, "Life is short. Eat dessert first." I have a different view on this. Anyone who has spent any time with me knows I'm not a fan of vegetables. I accept the fact that a well-rounded diet is beneficial to my health and longevity, so I will eat my veggies. But I will eat them first. Doing this allows me to get to the things I prefer and love knowing that I've completed the things I don't. I've learned to apply this same logic to work activities.

As we navigate our busy lives, it's easy to get overwhelmed by the number of tasks and responsibilities we must juggle. Prioritization is key to managing these demands effectively, and a simple rule of thumb to remember is to "eat your veggies first and save the best for last."

This means tackling your most challenging or unpleasant tasks first, while saving the more enjoyable or easy tasks for later. Here are some tips for implementing this approach to prioritization in your life.

Identify Your Priorities

Before you can prioritize your tasks, you need to know what your priorities are. Make a list of your goals and responsibilities, and then rank them in order of importance. This will help you identify which tasks you should tackle first.

Tackle Your Most Challenging Tasks First

As the saying goes, "eat your veggies first." This means tackling your most challenging or unpleasant tasks first thing in the morning when you have the most energy and focus. By completing these tasks early, you'll feel a sense of accomplishment and motivation that will carry you through the rest of your day.

Break Large Tasks into Smaller Ones

Large tasks can be overwhelming and difficult to tackle, so break them down into smaller, more manageable tasks. This will help you feel more in control and make it easier to prioritize each task.

Schedule Your Tasks

Once you've identified your priorities, create a schedule for tackling each task. This will help you stay on track and ensure that you're making progress towards your goals.

Save the Best for Last

Finally, save the best for last. After you've completed your most challenging tasks, reward yourself by tackling the more enjoyable or easy tasks. This will help you maintain your motivation and make your work more enjoyable.

Generally, prioritization is key to managing our busy lives effectively. By identifying our priorities, tackling our most challenging tasks first, breaking large tasks into smaller ones, scheduling our tasks, and saving the best for last, we can achieve our goals and feel a sense of accomplishment. So, remember to "eat your veggies first and save the best for last" when it comes to prioritization, and watch your productivity and success soar.

CHAPTER FOUR
TWO SIMPLE PHRASES FOR TIME MANAGEMENT: NOT ME, NOT NOW

With the fast pace of business only getting faster, human beings can only do so much. The demand our business puts on us pales in comparison to the demand we put on ourselves to maintain high standards and achieve desired outcomes. There just never seems to be enough time to keep up. An approach that has always helped me manage my time is to recognize my own constraints but to always be helpful to those in need and to only do those things I am capable of and have time to prepare for to be successful. I should note that this does not mean avoiding taking on new things, but rather only accept requests that fit your time and skills.

So, what is time management? The dictionary says that time management is the ability to use one's time effectively or productively. It involves a juggling act of the demands on a person from all aspects of life. Effective use of your time empowers you to decide what you're spending time on. There are tools and techniques to help manage time, but I have found that it starts with knowing what your capabilities, priorities and responsibilities are and avoiding taking on anything where you're not the best fit.

Time is a precious resource, and effective time management is essential for achieving success in any endeavor. In this chapter, we'll explore two simple phrases that can help you manage your time more effectively: "Not Me" and "Not Now."

But before I get into the approach to these phrases, I trust that you, dear reader, will know that the idea is to use the spirit of these phrases and not necessarily the actual words in practice. Use your best judgement.

"Not Me"

The phrase "Not Me" is a simple reminder to focus on your own capabilities, priorities, and responsibilities, rather than getting sidetracked by distractions or requests from others. It's easy to get caught up in other people's agendas, but by saying "Not Me," you can regain control of your time and focus on what's most important.

For example, if a colleague asks you to take on an additional task that isn't in line with your own capabilities, priorities, or responsibilities, you can simply say, "Not Me." This can be a polite way to decline the request and avoid taking on unnecessary work that could interfere with your own goals and deadlines.

"Not Now"

The phrase "Not Now" is a powerful tool for managing your time and staying focused on what's most important. It's easy to get distracted by interruptions or other urgent tasks, but by saying "Not Now," you can maintain your focus and keep your attention on the task at hand. For example, if you're working on an important project and someone interrupts you with an unrelated question or request, you can simply say, "Not Now." This can be a polite way to indicate that you're busy and can't be interrupted now, without being dismissive or rude.

Always be Helpful

Using these two simple phrases can help you manage your time more effectively and achieve your goals more efficiently. By focusing on your own priorities and responsibilities, and staying focused on the task at hand, you can avoid distractions and interruptions that can interfere with your productivity and success. Avoid saying; "It's not my job." You should also Always Be Helpful and ensure that your colleague knows who the best person is to assist them. By doing this you will still provide value and your colleague will appreciate you guiding them.

Let me provide a practical example of what this might look like when someone asks you to do something. Let's say someone comes to you on a Friday with a request to meet with a client first thing Monday, in Dallas, Texas, to review a business value assessment for a product that is being proposed. You realize quickly this is going to be a tough request to handle. For one thing, you live in San Diego, California and you have family obligations on Sunday afternoons. You also are not up to speed on the product in question. You have the choice to make every effort to learn the product, review the assessment and be in Dallas on Monday or you can help the person by finding either a better resource or negotiating a better day and time. You might say, "Hey, thanks for asking me to help but that's not me and there is not enough time for me to prepare. I am not the best person for this because of time constraints and product knowledge. Let me help you by recommending my colleague, who lives in Austin and is trained up." The interaction shows that you are not the right person at the right time for this request, but you offer to connect them with someone who is.

To summarize, "Not Me" and "Not Now" are two simple phrases that can help you manage your time more effectively and achieve your goals more efficiently. By using these phrases to maintain your focus and avoid distractions, you can improve your productivity and achieve success in any endeavor. Always be Helpful and provide value by guiding your colleagues. You might not be the right person at the right time, but you might know who is. As a manager you can use these phrases to delegate activities. Remember that as a manager you don't have to do everything, but you do have to make sure everything gets done. So, start using these phrases today and see the difference they can make!

CHAPTER FIVE
EIGHT DAYS A WEEK: THE BENEFITS OF WORKING EFFICIENTLY

What if I told you that it is possible to create more time? Or maybe it's possible to control time. That would be pretty cool, right? I believe that it is possible and that the key is efficiency.

Everyone has the same 24 hours in a day, 7 days a week. But what if you could have an extra day every week? By working efficiently, it's possible to create more time for yourself and accomplish more in less time. In this chapter, we'll explore how working efficiently is like having eight days a week.

Before we get to the benefits let's review what working efficiently means. The goal is to reach an optimal level of productivity. In my experience the two biggest enemies of efficiency are unplanned interruption and procrastination. You can control issues arising from procrastination and that starts with working on yourself. Using the principles outlined earlier in this guide; you can better organize and manage the time you allocate to your activities.

So, what does working efficiently look like? When it comes to planning and preparation, I start with something like; "what are the goals? or, how much time do I have?" I learned a long time ago that I find it very helpful to break things down into threes. Let's say I'm asked to pull together an initiative to refresh a sales engineering process and methodologies. I will look at the three core elements of priorities, programs, and problems. From there I can further break each of the elements down so I can tackle them. Using "Lists," I can organize the activities. Using "Nine Minutes Day," I can plan regularly. Applying the idea of "Eat Your Veggies First," I can set some priorities. And, using "Not Me, Not Now," I can do some time blocking and minimize distractions to ensure I have the time to complete my goals.

The more you apply the principles, in a way that works for you, the more comfortable you will become and the more productive you will be. As time goes on you will see the benefits of working efficiently which makes all this fulfilling. Or at least tolerable.

Now on to the benefits.

More Productive Time

When you work efficiently, you're able to get more done in less time. This means that you can accomplish more in a single day than you would otherwise. By optimizing your workflow and minimizing distractions, you can maximize your productive time and achieve your goals faster.

Less Stress

When you're constantly running behind schedule and struggling to keep up with your workload, it can be incredibly stressful. By working efficiently, you can reduce the amount of stress in your life. When you have more time to complete tasks, you're less likely to feel overwhelmed and stressed out.

More Opportunities

When you're able to get more done in less time, you'll have more opportunities to take on new projects and explore new interests. By being efficient with your time, you'll be able to pursue new opportunities without sacrificing the quality of your work or your personal life.

Improved Quality of Work

When you're rushing to complete tasks and struggling to keep up with your workload, the quality of your work can suffer. By working efficiently, you'll be able to devote more time and attention to each task, resulting in higher quality work. This can lead to greater satisfaction in your job and more recognition for your achievements.

Greater Work-Life Balance

When you're able to get more done in less time, you'll have more time to spend on your personal life. This can lead to a greater sense of balance between your work and personal life, reducing stress and improving overall well-being. By working efficiently, you can achieve your goals while also enjoying a fulfilling personal life. When you're able to complete your work more quickly, you'll have more time to spend on hobbies, exercise, and spending time with loved ones. This can lead to a happier, more balanced life.

Increased Efficiency and Effectiveness

By working efficiently, you'll become more effective at completing tasks and achieving your goals. You'll be able to prioritize your work and focus on what's most important, resulting in greater efficiency and productivity. This can lead to greater success in your career and personal life.

Improved Time Management Skills

Working efficiently requires strong time management skills. By focusing on optimizing your workflow and minimizing distractions, you'll develop better time management skills that can benefit you in all areas of your life. This can lead to greater success and fulfillment in your career and personal life.

Overall, it may be said, working efficiently is like having eight days a week. By applying the principles presented in chapters one through four, you can maximize your productive time and minimize distractions. This will allow you to achieve more in less time, reduce stress, and improve your overall well-being. By developing strong time management skills and focusing on what's most important, you can achieve your goals while also enjoying a fulfilling personal life.

CHAPTER SIX
BE PROACTIVE

In any business, customer satisfaction is important. When people and technology are involved, there is no question of whether there will be issues; it is a matter of when they will occur. When customer issues are approached proactively and with proper planning and preparation, a positive outcome is more readily available.

On an average day, we are actively engaged with more than a dozen projects involving thousands of people. When issues arise during our projects, there is a risk of negatively affecting our customer's business. Because of the high visibility of these activities, we often attempt to account for every process within our control, whether direct or indirect. Many problems are unique to a specific customer's business processes and are difficult to plan for mitigation, but if we use a proactive approach and provide general guidelines using a methodology that addresses many of the common pitfalls, we can get ahead of problems and manage through them.

One example of a common problem we face is when a component or a function of a software program fails it is sometimes difficult to locate the faulty code or process. Part of the problem is that many components are developed using shared or open-source code libraries. Error logging is often limited for these libraries. When the error logging is lacking the necessary details to focus in on the cause of failures, we often find it difficult to establish the proof needed to hold people accountable for their activities. Some people involved will attempt to deflect any responsibility for assisting with resolution.

In a reactive approach, you might find yourself attempting to expose the failures on the part of the customer or other parties involved. You might try to point out their missteps with their responsibilities, and then respond to their reaction. For example, your response may be that whatever the issue, it is not your fault. Another response might be that there is nothing that could have been done to change the outcome. Reactively, it might be suggested that the issue would not have been experienced if there had been more diligence in planning and managing the processes.

As you contemplate the possible customer situations, consider what events might occur and develop into problems that will require resolution. Stopping to consider all the options available as you face new challenges begins with knowing, whatever our approach, it is your decision to work together. We are free to choose how we will respond to the issues we encounter and affect the outcome that results. Once we have identified the issue, we can then move forward with the steps necessary to find resolution. I have found that it is best to set aside how I feel in the moment and participate in the steps toward resolution.

Understanding each area of impact that you can influence will contribute to a successful result. Identifying what your role is in the issue from both the cause and the effect will allow you to respond in a way that shows a willingness to accept responsibility and positively influence the outcome. Showing flexibility in accepting feedback and ideas from others in creating solutions encourages a team approach. Being mindful to choose the language, expressions, and physical response to those you're working with will demonstrate commitment to a positive solution.

Keeping customers happy is important to our business. Knowing how we react to trouble when it appears is as much a part of remediation for the customer as resolving the issue itself. Working with customers in a proactive way will help to manage issues before they begin.

CHAPTER SEVEN
MANAGEMENT STYLES APPLIED

I think it goes without saying that all organizations, regardless of size, require management to achieve its stated goals. I am convinced this applies to individuals as well. Throughout my career I have had the opportunity to validate that assertion time and again. In addition to drawing on this experience, this chapter will review a set of management styles, briefly define them, provide an example of each, and outline the overall approach for the one I have adopted. Maybe you too will identify your style or find one to incorporate.

As I set out to research management styles, I decided to use the Internet as my primary tool. I further decided to limit my search to the most common of management styles: democratic, autocratic, and laissez-faire. Among those not included in this review, but worthy of noting are bureaucratic, permissive, facilitative, objective seeking, and crisis management.

The approach in defining each management style will be to provide a commonly accepted definition, in this case, as found on www.answers.com. As a follow up to each definition, I will provide a personal example from my career to demonstrate each style.

The first style to define is the democratic or participative management style. A democratic management style is defined as one where the manager allows the employees to take part in the decision-making process. A manager that uses this style encourages participation from key personnel. At one of my former companies, a senior leader used this style to facilitate discussion on various topics such as new products and services offerings, company functions, and solutions to operational issues. His method of pursuing his objective of soliciting input was most often by casual and seemingly impromptu one-on-one conversations with select personnel. He sometimes surrounded himself with a trusted group of employees, some with management roles, to provide input and insight into items of concern. The outcome of these sessions occasionally caused disjointed and disconnected working relationships by creating unnecessary competition. Used properly this style can allow you to receive the information needed to execute a plan. But caution should be used with this style to avoid creating an atmosphere where favoritism and manipulation affect how the participants interact.

Not Me, Not Now. Mastering Your Time, Your Team, and Yourself
A Simple Guide to Effective Management

Autocratic or authoritarian management is defined as a style in which one person makes all the decisions, sets all objectives, allocates all tasks, and expects the staff to do exactly as required. A former colleague and I shared management duties during the time we had been working at the company. We started there at roughly the same time and managed several areas of the business from customer engagements to operations. This colleague sometimes used the autocratic management style. His approach was to layout programs where he set the individual staff objectives and made decisions with little or no input. In my experience, this management style can limit the results of the objectives of the company and the employees. Although in some ways, it serves the objectives of this manager. One of the pitfalls is that staff members don't feel connected to the vision. This might lead to stifled creativity and negative morale. One benefit of this style appears to be the speed at which some activities can be accomplished because the manager requires no consulting and makes all decisions. In some types of business, the autocratic style has its place and can be of value, but it should be used sparingly and balanced with other styles.

A management style where the manager allows the staff to act on whatever must be done and provides little input on direction or control is called laissez-faire or delegative. Over the years, my management style had been to set an agenda or direction and allow my staff to work toward the objectives. I had found that most professionals appreciate the freedom to use their own judgment in performing their duties. If I concern myself less with the "how" something is accomplished, and more on the outcome, the parties involve feel more fulfilled and innovation springs up. In most cases, this management style has served me well in that my hiring practices have allowed me to choose staff members that require little supervision, are self-motivated, and understand their roles and responsibilities.

At one point in my career, I received a promotion to Vice President of Professional Services. This promotion gave me an opportunity to implement a new approach to my management style. As I studied the various styles and methods, I observed that a combination of autocratic, democratic, and laissez-faire management styles seemed to work best. By surrounding myself with reliable colleagues, I used a democratic process of recommending, reviewing, refining, and planning the implementation of programs and procedures that contribute to business objectives while providing the opportunity for individuals to meet personal and professional objectives. As their manager, I set the objective and the desired outcome of this process using the laissez-faire approach to programs and procedures decided on by the committee in a way where staff members can work toward their goals with little interruption. I would follow up and support the staff through coaching and by making the tough decisions when needed.

One of the first changes I made to the organizational structure was to create two new positions, Managing Consultant and Solutions Architect. Within the current structure, I had assigned these roles to six staff members, four Managing Consultants and two Solutions Architects. The primary purpose of these roles was to assist me in market research, staff development, and customer satisfaction programs. Once the information was collected and an approach for each area had been defined, I allowed the staff to work toward assigned objectives.

As part of these new assignments, I outlined the authority each of the roles had in daily operations. One thing that had been lacking at the company was a clear definition of responsibilities. As I was developing as a manager, and given the opportunity, my plan was to implement a system with more consistency and require intentional measurements with appropriate accountability. With my new role, I started the process by scheduling a series of open discussions where the Managing Consultants had the chance to review their roles with each other and work through what is working and not working. My intention was to use this meeting to build strong relationships between these people to create a culture that allows for better teaming. I also instituted a regular meeting between the two Solutions Architects with the purpose of encouraging thought leadership from our most talented technologists. I believed that with a little coordination and encouragement, using the democratic style, the Managing Consultants would be motivated and empowered to make good decisions in how our business operates. I further believed that with little facilitation, using the laissez-faire style, the Solutions Architects would provide valuable advice on future trends and direction for products and services offerings.

A Simple Guide to Effective Management

The value of management to a company can only be realized through the execution of the activities that meet the business objectives. It has been my experience that the management style used must contain an element of flexibility to be successful. A hard-lined approach of the autocratic manager, while appropriate for some organizations, does not lend itself to good customer satisfaction as required by product and professional services companies. There is often not enough time to employ the democratic approach to management and this approach may have a negative impact on services utilization and revenue. The laissez-faire style does not work well with staff that requires frequent attention from management. Overall, it appears that a blended approach works best given the varying job functions and personality types. Throughout the course of my career, I have worked to find a balance between autocratic, democratic, and laissez-faire styles of management and this approach has served me well.

CHAPTER EIGHT
LEADING FROM ANYWHERE

The following is a summary of a paper that I had written for school years ago. It is basically a book review but with a focus on lessons learned and the principles I worked into my career journey and leadership development. I also highlight how the book helped me reinforce personal growth and practical application. I encourage you to read the book from John C. Maxwell, "The 360-Degree Leader: Developing your influence from anywhere in the organization." I learned that leading from anywhere in an organization is possible and will have a positive impact on you and your colleagues.

I used to believe that leadership primarily originated from the top of an organization. However, my perspective shifted after reading "The 360-Degree Leader: Developing your influence from anywhere in the organization." This book taught me that leadership can emerge at various levels within a company. In my career, I often found myself wishing for more control or authority in certain situations. Upon reflection, I realized that I possessed the necessary control and authority to achieve the desired objectives. I simply had to develop a plan, build support, and act.

In "The 360-Degree Leader," Maxwell delves into the myths, challenges, and principles of leadership from different positions within an organization. He provides practical solutions for each myth and challenge presented in the book. The seven sections of the book cover topics such as leading from the middle, challenges faced by middle leaders, and the principles of a 360-Degree Leader. The book emphasizes the importance of influence and offers insights on leading up, down, and across the organization.

One of the key lessons from the book is that leadership is not solely dependent on one's position but rather on the influence one has developed at different levels of an organization. Maxwell outlines five levels of leadership: position, permission, production, people development, and personhood. These levels illustrate why people choose to follow a leader and how experience at each level contributes to a leader's influence.

The book also addresses the challenges middle leaders face, including tensions, ineffective leaders, multiple roles, ego, and championing a vision created by others. Maxwell provides practical solutions for these challenges, guiding readers on how to navigate them effectively.

The principles of a 360-Degree Leader focus on leading up, down, and across the organization. Leading up involves self-leadership, lightening the load for superiors, and going beyond mere management to true leadership. Leading down emphasizes availability, developing team members, and transferring the organizational vision. Leading across requires caring for peers, learning from them, and contributing value to their success.

The book emphasizes the value that 360-Degree Leaders bring to organizations, such as the effectiveness of a leadership team, the need for leaders at all levels, and the development of better leaders from the middle to the top. The final section is dedicated to top leaders, urging them to create an environment that fosters the emergence of 360-Degree Leaders. Maxwell provides a list of activities, known as the "Daily Dozen," which top leaders can implement to support and unleash leadership potential within the organization.

During the time I first read "The 360-Degree Leader" I had a corner office with a nice view of both outside and the operational area of our firm. After accepting the position of Vice President, I was reluctant to move into this office because I feared my team would begin to view me as the boss and not the enabler, mentor, and coach I wanted to be. There is something about the location of your office and title on your business card that affects the way people interact with you. I experienced something I had hoped to avoid. Colleagues that I shared a close relationship with minimized their openness the further up the management ladder I climbed.

To reclaim the business relationships, I desired between my team members and me, and to apply what I was learning, I implemented a study group using "The 360-Degree Leader" book. My intension was to encourage others who were leading our organization to use the same language and share common objectives. Some on the team were reluctant to commit to the study at first. Others showed excitement by the idea that we would be working and growing together in a professional environment. I discovered that some of the team members are natural leaders and these concepts come very easily to them. Others have difficulty accepting their role as leaders within the company. They struggled with their current position as a career decision but believed learning with the group would provide a good experience. One of the greatest values I found from this activity was confirming each leader's ability and in doing so confirming my own. This supported the behaviors I desired from the team and had encouraged a new openness that in turn allowed for better communication and a more positive work environment.

Over the years I have had several opportunities to exercise leading in various directions. Most of the time these experiences were beneficial and provided for unexpected career advancement. At one point I was in an individual contributor role as a technical leader. I was enjoying not having any direct reports and was focusing on a new product area. As I was getting my arms around the position, my manager was struggling with a new team and how to manage it. As we discussed the situation, and I began to understand the challenges, I saw a chance to use the principle of "leading up" and lightening the load of my manager. So, I offered to take on the additional role of managing this new team. Doing so allowed me to expand my skills, as well as my influence, by leading a new area of our business. By being open to taking on something new and helping my manager meet the demands of the business, I became known as someone who can be counted on. And this was very fulfilling.

Overall, "The 360-Degree Leader" has profoundly impacted my understanding of leadership. Of the many concepts and principles learned in my studies, most valuable to me has been developing the discipline to take advantage of the resources available to me as a manager and leader. This assignment, and in particular this book, reminded me that good leadership is an ongoing development idea and not a status to achieve. Maxwell says, "Leading better from the middle is a sure sign that these issues resonate with you." What I discovered from this book has lasted throughout my career and life in general. I further find that a key underlying principle, the zest of the book if you will, is to be an effective leader means to remove your selfish ambitions and focus on supporting others. This has become a driving force for me both personally and professionally and I have found that I am not only a better leader, employee, father, and husband but in fact receive an indescribable amount of blessing from seeing others do well.

CHAPTER NINE
SIX THINGS I LEARNED FROM NEHEMIAH

Early in my management career I didn't have much formal training or education in how to manage myself, but there I was being asked to manage other people. As luck, or maybe divine intervention, would have it, we were reading the story of Nehemiah at our church. Our study was focused on how Nehemiah managed his time, people, and resources to respond to his calling. I found this information timely and picked up a few things that I still use today. Most of the insights I briefly outline here are from the first 8 chapters of the Book of Nehemiah. I encourage you to read the text yourself. It's good history and will show you how much can be accomplished even against seemingly impossible odds.

Nehemiah was a great leader in the Bible who managed to rebuild the walls of Jerusalem despite facing various challenges. His story offers valuable lessons about leadership and management that can be applied in today's workplace. In this chapter, we'll explore six things I learned about management from Nehemiah.

Have a Vision

Nehemiah had a clear vision of what he wanted to achieve - rebuilding the walls of Jerusalem. He communicated this vision to his team and worked tirelessly to make it a reality. A clear and compelling vision is essential for motivating and inspiring your team and keeping everyone aligned towards a common goal.

Develop a Plan

Nehemiah developed a detailed plan for rebuilding the walls of Jerusalem, including assessing the damage, organizing the workforce, and assigning specific tasks. A well-crafted plan can help you manage your resources effectively, anticipate potential challenges, and ensure that everyone is working towards the same goal.

Lead by Example

Nehemiah was a hands-on leader who worked alongside his team to rebuild the walls. He didn't just delegate tasks - he rolled up his sleeves and got to work. Leading by example can help build trust and credibility with your team and demonstrate your commitment to achieving your vision.

Overcome Obstacles

Nehemiah faced numerous obstacles while rebuilding the walls of Jerusalem, including opposition from neighboring tribes and internal conflict among his team. However, he remained persistent and found creative solutions to overcome these challenges. As a manager, it's important to anticipate and address obstacles and find ways to navigate around them.

Celebrate Success

When the walls of Jerusalem were finally rebuilt, Nehemiah celebrated the success with his team. Celebrating success can help build morale and motivation and create a positive and rewarding work environment.

Prioritize Personal Growth

Finally, Nehemiah prioritized his own personal growth and development. He was committed to improving his leadership skills and building his knowledge and expertise. As a manager, it's important to prioritize your own personal growth and development, as well as that of your team.

I realize that these lessons aren't unique to Nehemiah, but his story offers valuable insights about leadership and management that can be applied in today's workplace. By having a clear vision, developing a plan, leading by example, overcoming obstacles, celebrating success, and prioritizing personal growth, you can become a more effective and successful manager.

CHAPTER TEN
MANAGE, COACH, OR MENTOR. A TUGBOAT STORY

Some years ago, I was in a small group and the leader asked an ice breaker question. "If you could be any type of boat, what would that be?" After a little thought I said, "I think of myself as a tugboat." I was asked to explain that a bit and then went on to talk about how I could be a battleship, a cruise ship or something like that but that I found I am most comfortable being in a role where I can help people navigate to where they need to be. Tugboats are specially equipped to play a crucial role in the safe and efficient movement of other vessels. I am fulfilled by helping others realize their potential and am also specially equipped in the roles of manager, coach, and mentor.

Knowing the role, you play, and when to play it, in supporting your business is important to developing expectations and relationships. As a manager you will play a different role based on the need of the individual. Being accommodating and flexible is important to ensuring you are helping your staff meet their goals and succeed in their jobs.

Managing, coaching, and mentoring are three distinct approaches to supporting and developing someone's professional growth and success. While there is often some overlap, each approach has its unique characteristics.

Managing involves oversight and direction of the work of an employee to ensure that they meet their assigned obligations. Managers usually have formal authority over their subordinates, and their role involves assigning tasks, providing feedback, evaluating performance, and making decisions that impact the employee's work.

Coaching is more about working one-on-one to improve individual performance, develop new skills, and achieve their goals. A coach provides guidance and support through a collaborative process, helping the person to identify their strengths and weaknesses, set realistic objectives, and create a plan to achieve them. Coaches typically ask questions to help the person discover their own solutions and build their confidence and abilities.

Mentoring involves sharing their knowledge and expertise with another person. Sometimes mentors have more experience, but this doesn't have to always be the case. The mentor acts as a role model, advisor, and teacher, offering guidance, feedback, and support to help the mentee develop their skills, knowledge, and abilities. Mentors often share their own experiences and insights to help the mentee gain a broader perspective on their profession and career.

In summary, while managing focuses on directing and overseeing an employee's work, coaching is more about helping them improve and develop their skills, while mentoring is about sharing knowledge and experience to support someone's long-term professional growth. I should note here that not all managers make good coaches or mentors. And as a manager, you should be mindful that there may be others who can play these roles to help your team members. As you help your team navigate everything from their day jobs to their career aspirations, you can take on the role, like that of a tugboat, to help ensure they move in a safe and efficient direction to meet their goals.

CHAPTER ELEVEN
IT'S NOT EASY BEING GREEN: TIPS FOR NEW MANAGERS

I still remember the first job I had as a manager. Facing my new team for the first time was both exhilarating and terrifying. I had been promoted to manage the team where I was a member. I remember thinking, "They're going to realize I have no idea what I'm doing." Ultimately that wasn't the case and things worked out.

Throughout this guide I have covered several ways to manage effectively so I won't belabor these points below. I would encourage you to work these tips into your regular activities and set reminders to continuously improve on them.

Starting a new job as a manager can be daunting, especially if you're new to the role. You may feel like you're in over your head and struggling to keep up with the demands of your new position. But remember, it's not easy being green. Here are some tips for new managers to help you navigate this challenging but rewarding journey.

Ask for Help

It's okay to ask for help, especially when you're starting out as a new manager. Don't be afraid to reach out to your colleagues or mentor for guidance and support. They can offer valuable insights and advice that can help you become a more effective manager.

I want to highlight here that it is important to identify one or two manager mentors to meet with regularly. Be intentional about the topics you cover during each session and take notes. Keep track of the insights gained through these discussions and how you used them in your management approach. This will help you get the most out of the time with your mentor.

Help can also be found in a few management resources like books and online training courses. Below is a list of books that I consumed over the years.

"The 7 Habits of Highly Effective People: Powerful Lessons in Personal Change" by Stephen R. Covey

"The 360 Degree Leader: Developing Your Influence from Anywhere in the Organization" by John C. Maxwell

"The 21 Irrefutable Laws of Leadership" by John C. Maxwell

"Built to Last: Successful Habits of Visionary Companies" by Jim Collins

"Good to Great: Why Some Companies Make the Leap...And Others Don't" by Jim Collins

"The New One Minute Manager" by Kenneth Blanchard & Spencer Johnson

"Who Moved My Cheese?: An A-Mazing Way to Deal with Change in Your Work and in Your Life" by Spencer Johnson

Learn from Mistakes

Mistakes are inevitable, especially when you're new to a role. Instead of beating yourself up over your mistakes, learn from them. Reflect on what went wrong and how you can avoid making the same mistake in the future. Commit to improvement. Use your mistakes as an opportunity to grow and improve as a manager.

Build Relationships

Critical to your success as a manager is how you relate to others. It's about people. Building strong relationships with your team and colleagues is crucial for success as a manager. Take the time to get to know your team members and understand their strengths, weaknesses, and goals. Building strong relationships can help build trust, improve communication, and create a positive and productive work environment.

Communicate Clearly

Clear communication is essential for effective management. Make sure you communicate your expectations, goals, and priorities clearly and regularly to your team. Encourage open communication and be receptive to feedback from your team.

Prioritize Time Management

As a new manager, you'll likely have a lot on your plate. Prioritize your time effectively by focusing on the most important tasks and delegating to your team when appropriate. Don't be afraid to say no to non-essential tasks or to delegate to others when needed. Be sure to go back and read chapters two through five of this guide.

Stay Positive

Finally, remember to stay positive. Starting a new role can be challenging, but it can also be incredibly rewarding. Stay focused on your goals and maintain a positive attitude. If you feel yourself starting to feel weighed down and your negativity growing, find an outlet for it. Avoid sharing or directing negative attitudes toward your team. Be sure to celebrate your successes and learn from your failures and remember that in most cases things will get easier as you gain more experience.

Generally, being a new manager is challenging, but it's also an opportunity for growth and development. By asking for help, learning from your mistakes, building relationships, communicating clearly, prioritizing time management, and staying positive, you can become a successful and effective manager. As we wrap up this chapter and move on to the next, remember, it's not easy being green, but with time and experience, you'll become more confident and skilled in your role.

CHAPTER TWELVE
SEVEN DEADLY MANAGER SINS

It is commonly said that employees don't quit jobs, they quit managers. I'm not sure I completely agree with this statement, but it certainly has some truth to it. In my experience the opposite is equally true. Employees stay with managers even when the job is difficult or less than fun. How you treat the people on your team, especially when times are tough, will have an impact on your business.

As a manager, it's important to lead your team in a positive direction. However, there are some common mistakes that can lead to negative consequences. These mistakes are often referred to as the "Seven Deadly Management Sins." There are a few articles available on the Internet and I encourage you to search for them for additional consideration. Because I am writing from experiences, here are seven sins, that I have committed, and some tips on how to avoid them.

Sin #1: Micromanagement

Micromanagement is number one for a reason. It is a common mistake made by many managers and one that most of fall back to when things aren't going as we expect. When you micromanage, you're overly involved in the day-to-day tasks of your team members. This can make them feel undervalued and can hinder their creativity and productivity. To avoid micromanagement, trust your team members to complete tasks on their own. Provide guidance and support but allow them the freedom to do their work. I've said this before, let adult professionals be. You are often better off focusing on what needs to be done and not on how it's done.

Sin #2: Lack of Communication

Communication is essential in any workplace. As a manager, it's your responsibility to ensure that your team members are well-informed and understand their role within the organization. Failure to communicate effectively can lead to misunderstandings and mistakes. To avoid this sin, be clear and concise in your communication. It is very important to pay special attention to how and what you're communicating during times of high urgency and pressure. Use multiple channels to communicate important information, confirm clarity, and encourage feedback from your team members.

Sin #3: Lack of Accountability

As a manager, it's important to hold your team members accountable for their actions. When you fail to do so, you're sending a message that mistakes and poor performance are acceptable. We all mess up from time to time, that's understandable. So be sure to focus on correcting the problem and not tearing down the person. Most situations are an opportunity for improvement and building trust. To avoid this sin, set clear expectations and consequences for your team members. Hold them accountable for their actions, but also provide support and resources to help them succeed.

Sin #4: Favoritism

Favoritism is a common mistake made by many managers. I'm guilty of this. Look, sometimes we just get along better with some than others. That's just human nature. But, when you play favorites, you risk creating a toxic work environment that can lead to resentment and mistrust. To avoid this sin, treat all team members fairly and equally. Give permission to your team members to hold you accountable. Recognize and reward good performance, but don't show favoritism.

Sin #5: Lack of Trust

Trust is essential in any workplace. When you fail to trust your team members, you're creating an environment of suspicion and negativity. And these attitudes can have lasting impact to your business. To avoid this sin, trust your team members to do their jobs. Remember, they're professionals. Prove yourself a trustworthy person, provide them with the resources and support they need to succeed, but also give them the freedom to make decisions and take risks. In my experience when you trust your team some amazing things will happen. Trust me.

Sin #6: Lack of Empathy

I must confess that this sin was particularly difficult for me. Over the years I had to learn how process what I was observing in others. What I learned was, empathy is the ability to understand and share the feelings of others. Everyone should have this ability, but as a manager, it's important to show empathy to your team members. When you fail to do so, you're creating a work environment that lacks compassion and understanding. If you're team thinks you don't care this will be reciprocated and even spread. To avoid this sin, take the time to listen to your team members and understand their concerns. Show compassion and understanding and provide support when needed. And be sure to follow up and follow through.

Sin #7: Lack of Vision

And last, a lack of vision can lead to confusion and uncertainty within your team. As a manager, it's important to have a clear vision for your team and the organization. This vision should be communicated to your team members and should guide their work. To avoid this sin, take the time to develop a clear vision for, and in some cases, with your team and communicate it effectively.

These Seven Deadly Manager Sins can have negative consequences for both you and your team. Be intentional and avoid these sins by, focusing on building trust, communication, accountability, and empathy within your team. By doing so, you'll create a positive work environment that encourages productivity and success.

CHAPTER THIRTEEN
YOUR REPUTATION AND RELATIONSHIPS: PROTECT THEM!

One of the biggest issues that you run into when working with people is that inevitably they get to know you. And let's face it nobody is perfect. The more you interact with people the more they see your flaws and the more they see your flaws the more willing they are to express how those flaws are not agreeable to them, even if it's not directly to you. If you let your flaws show too often you ultimately get a bad reputation. To balance this, I've learned that building a strong reputation coupled with strong relationships helps to recover from my flaws, missteps, and bad days.

Your professional reputation is one of the most valuable assets you have in your career. A good reputation can open doors and create opportunities, while a bad reputation can limit your potential and harm your career prospects. In this chapter, we'll explore how to avoid developing a bad professional reputation and bad relationships in the workplace.

Be Honest and Transparent

Honesty and transparency are key components of a good professional reputation. It's important to be truthful in your interactions with colleagues and clients, and to avoid any misrepresentations or deceitful behavior. If you make a mistake or have an issue to address, it's best to be upfront and transparent about it, rather than trying to cover it up.

Communicate Effectively

Effective communication is essential for building good relationships in the workplace. This includes both listening and expressing yourself clearly and respectfully. It's important to be attentive to others' needs and concerns, and to communicate in a way that is professional and constructive.

Be Reliable and Consistent

Reliability and consistency are also important for building a good reputation in the workplace. If you make a commitment or promise, it's essential to follow through and deliver on your word. Consistently meeting deadlines and delivering high-quality work can help establish your reputation as a reliable and valuable team member.

Avoid Gossip and Negative Behaviors

Gossip and negative behaviors can quickly tarnish your professional reputation and harm your relationships with colleagues. It's important to avoid engaging in gossip or negative talk about others, and to maintain a positive and respectful attitude towards your colleagues.

Seek Feedback and Growth

Finally, seeking feedback and opportunities for growth can help you continue to develop your professional reputation and relationships. By seeking feedback from colleagues and supervisors, you can identify areas for improvement and work to address any concerns or issues.

Additionally, seeking out opportunities for learning and growth can demonstrate your commitment to personal and professional development.

In conclusion, building a good professional reputation and developing strong, positive relationships in the workplace takes time and effort. By being honest and transparent, communicating effectively, being reliable and consistent, avoiding negative behaviors, and seeking feedback and growth, you can establish a positive reputation and build strong relationships with your colleagues. Remember, your reputation is one of your most valuable assets - protect it and nurture it, and it will serve you well throughout your career.

CHAPTER FOURTEEN
REINVENT YOURSELF, REGULARLY

In today's fast-paced and ever-changing work environment, especially in the information technology industry, it's important to be adaptable and flexible. One way to do this is by regularly reinventing yourself professionally. In this chapter, we'll explore the importance of reinventing yourself professionally and how to do it effectively.

Keeping Up with Changing Demands

The job market is constantly changing, and so are the demands of employers. To stay relevant and in-demand, it's important to be adaptable and willing to learn new skills. Regularly reinventing yourself professionally can help you stay current with the latest industry trends and demands and position yourself for new and exciting opportunities.

Avoiding Stagnation

Stagnation is a common problem in many careers. When you're doing the same thing day in and day out, it's easy to become complacent and lose your passion for your work. Reinventing yourself professionally can help you avoid stagnation by providing new challenges and opportunities for growth. It can also help you stay engaged and motivated in your work.

Enhancing Your Skill Set

Reinventing yourself professionally can also enhance your skill set and make you a more valuable employee. By learning new skills and taking on new challenges, you can broaden your expertise and become more versatile. This can make you more attractive to employers and increase your earning potential.

Building Resilience

Finally, regularly reinventing yourself professionally can help you build resilience and adaptability. When you're constantly learning and growing, you become better equipped to handle challenges and overcome obstacles. This can help you navigate changes in the job market and remain competitive throughout your career.

In conclusion, regularly reinventing yourself professionally is essential for staying relevant, avoiding stagnation, enhancing your skill set, and building resilience. Whether it's taking on new challenges, learning new skills, or exploring new industries, there are many ways to reinvent yourself professionally. Embrace the opportunity to learn and grow, and don't be afraid to step outside your comfort zone. By doing so, you can position yourself for long-term success and fulfillment in your career.

SUMMARY

In this guide, we've explored basic management principles that can help individuals and organizations achieve their goals and objectives. We've discussed the importance of effective organization, time management, the importance of self-management, prioritization, and management styles, among other key topics.

Effective organization and time management is essential for building strong relationships and achieving shared goals. We've discussed the importance of setting boundaries for yourself so you can focus on your capabilities that are important to you. Leading from anywhere in an organization starts with leading yourself effectively.

Prioritization is another crucial aspect of effective management. We've explored how to identify requests that can be managed through ensuring the right person is engaged at the right time. Sometimes that may not be you. Work to always be helpful and ensure the request has the right resource but avoid putting yourself in a losing situation.

We've also discussed the importance of setting goals and objectives, and how to develop and implement effective plans to achieve them. Using lists and being intentional about taking time to plan daily is a critical part of maintaining personal organization and dare I say some sanity.

One of the most impactful discoveries of my management career was learning the various styles of management and observing how managers use them, or not, in the real world. It may be obvious, but most managers don't adhere to their core style in every situation and often adjust to accommodate the different people and personalities they engage. Understanding your core management style will help you better understand yourself and those around you.

Being able to reinvent yourself is a great way to uncover opportunities for personal and professional development. Change is inevitable. Being prepared for that change is important and you can take control of most situations by being flexible and willing to take on new things and learn new ways.

Overall, the principles and strategies discussed in this guide can be applied in any organizational or personal context to improve communication, delegation, motivation, decision making, and overall performance. By adopting these basic management and leadership principles, individuals and organizations can achieve their goals and objectives more effectively and efficiently, and ultimately succeed in their endeavors. And, when all else fails, manage yourself well and the rest will often fall into place.

ACKNOWLEDGEMENT

It would be impossible to recognize and thank the countless people that have shaped me over the years. For the purposes of brevity, I would like to acknowledge and thank those who have been invaluable in the creation of this book.

First, I thank my wife, Stephanie, for her never-ending patience, unconditional support, and willingness to review and edit my work, as well as challenge my thinking.

Many thanks to my review team of Todd Condit, Chip Crane, and Joe Daw. Your feedback and insights were helpful in keeping the content clear and applicable to readers.

Lastly, I would like to thank all my colleagues who over the years have had such a positive impact on me. Our interactions have encouraged my continual growth and made for an enriching career.

Made in the USA
Columbia, SC
26 September 2023